Be a FOSSIL Hunter

by Ian MacDonald

illustrated by Elif Balta Parks

OXFORD
UNIVERSITY PRESS

Sasha and Ben are at the beach.
“Hey, look at this stone!” yells Ben.

“It’s a seashell,” says Sasha.

“It’s a fossil,” says Granny Madge.

"We could start a collection," says Ben.

"How would we know what to look for?" asks Sasha.

Mary Anning was a fossil hunter. She started collecting fossils when she was a girl.

Mary Anning

Mary Anning found this Dimorphodon fossil. She found it on a beach in Dorset in 1828.

Fossils come in all shapes and sizes. A fossil could be many things. Even a **prehistoric** footprint!

Most fossils are found near water. A good place to look is near lakes or rivers. You can also find fossils at the beach.

This is an ammonite. It's the shell of a sea creature that lived long ago. After thousands of years, the shell turned to stone.

These sharks' teeth are thousands of years old. These creatures are the relations of sharks that we see today.

We can learn a lot from just a few bones.

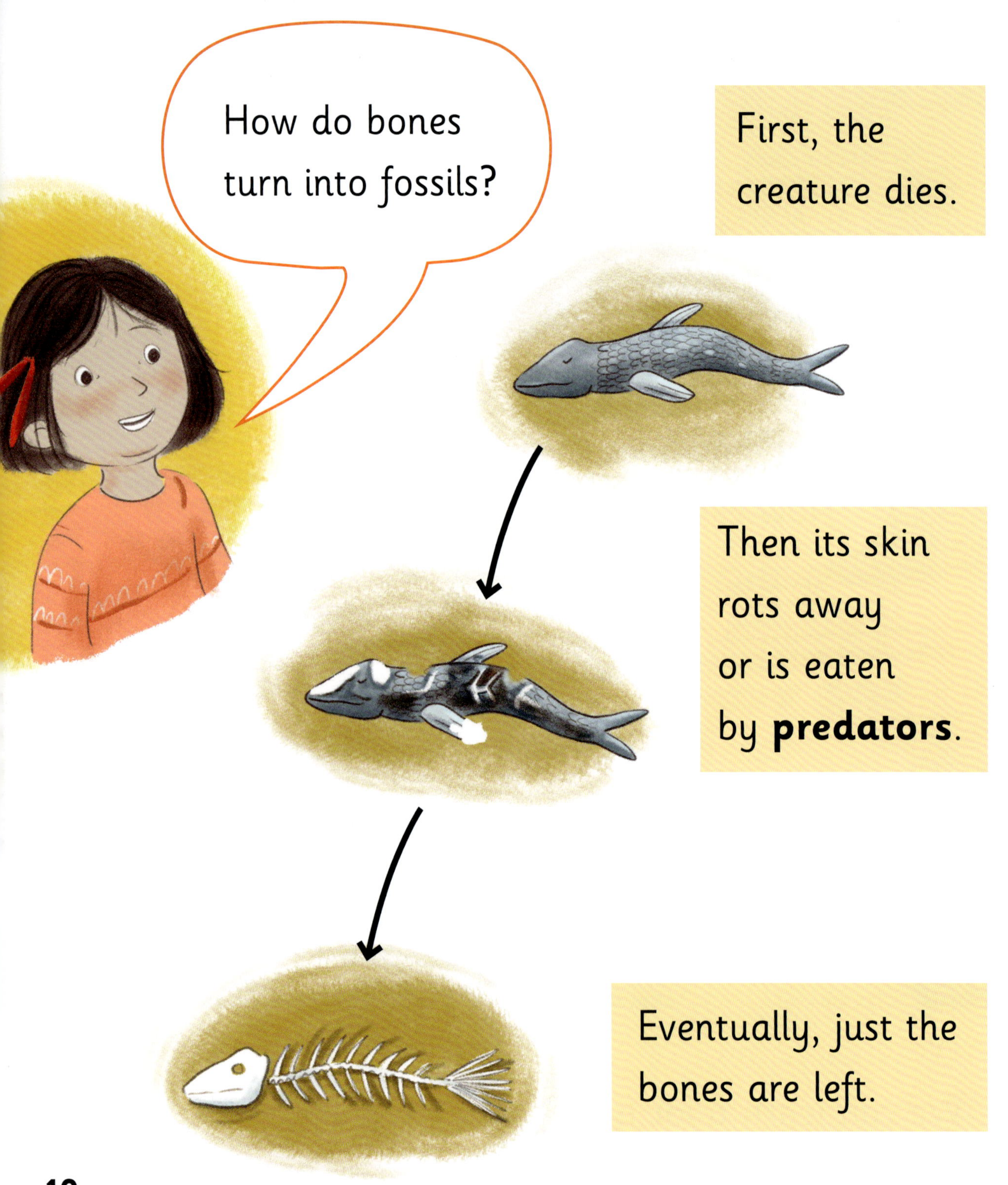

First, the creature dies.

Then its skin rots away or is eaten by **predators**.

Eventually, just the bones are left.

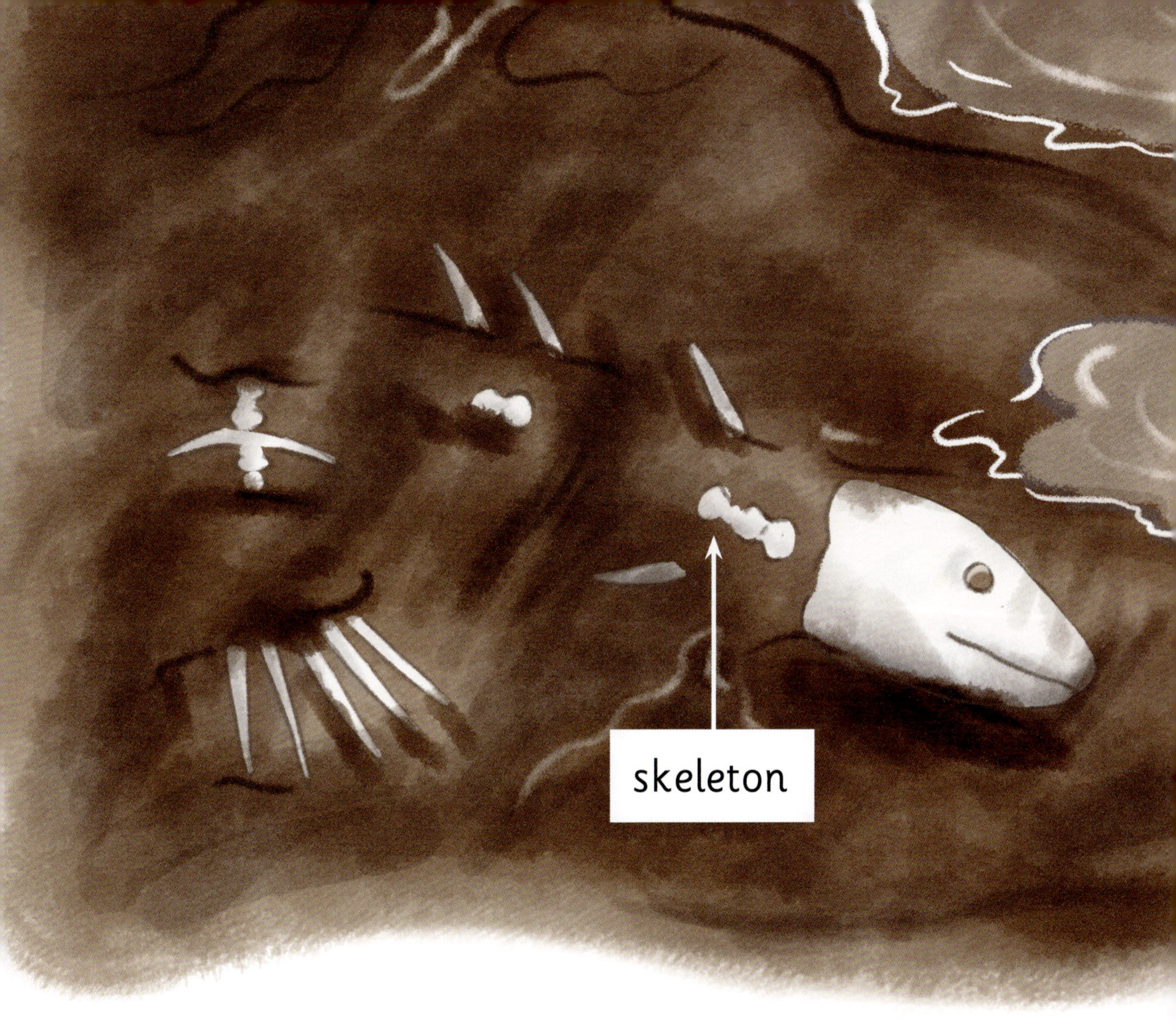

Layers of mud and sand pile up on the skeleton. Water seeps in, too. All this weight puts extreme **pressure** on the bones.

Mud and water form a **chemical reaction**. In time, the bones turn to stone. Fossils can tell us a lot about these prehistoric beasts.

The skull of the T Rex is large. It was designed to crush its **prey**.

The frill on this triceratops was helpful for protection. Its huge horns were useful in a fight. However, it was no match for a T Rex.

This creature wore bony plates to protect it. A boulder-shaped club on its tail kept predators away.

Over time, the skin of these prehistoric beasts has been lost. We now think most had feathers like a bird.

The **fossilized** dung of these prehistoric creatures is useful. It leaves clues about what they ate.

How do you hunt for a fossil? First, know where to look! Special maps help you find where the oldest rocks are.

Weather can wear away the rock. Some **fragments** might show up. Start looking!

Some fossils are underground. Fossil hunters might need to use **mechanical** diggers.

When you are near the fossil, work carefully. A trowel helps scrape away the dirt. Now get excited! You've found your fossil.

“I’m going to be a fossil hunter when I grow up!” cries Sasha.

“That’s my ambition, too!” adds Ben.

Make a Fossil

1. Place some clay into a plastic pot.
2. Press down a shell to leave a print.
3. Scoop in a mixture of **plaster of Paris**.
4. Let it dry, then find your fossil!

Glossary

chemical reaction: when one thing reacts to another, to form something new

fossilized: turned into a fossil

fragments: tiny pieces that have broken off something

mechanical: worked by a motor

plaster of Paris: a thick, white liquid that sets to become hard

predators: creatures that hunt other creatures for food

prehistoric: a very long time ago, before people wrote things down

pressure: the force with which one thing pushes against another

prey: a creature hunted for food

Index